Pebble® Plus

Earth and Space Science

Exploring Space

by David Conrad

CAPSTONE PRESS
a capstone imprint

Pebble Plus is published by Capstone Press,
151 Good Counsel Drive, P.O. Box 669, Mankato, Minnesota 56002.
www.capstonepub.com

Books published by Capstone Press are manufactured with paper
containing at least 10 percent post-consumer waste.

Library of Congress Cataloging-in-Publication Data
Conrad, David (David J.), 1967–
 Exploring space / by David Conrad.
  p. cm. — (Pebble plus: Earth and space science)
 Includes bibliographical references and index.
 Summary: "Simple text and full-color photos present information about the past and future of space exploration"—
Provided by publisher.
 ISBN 978-1-4296-6810-1 (library binding) — ISBN 978-1-4296-7139-2 (paperback)
 1. Outer space—Exploration—Juvenile literature. I. Title. II. Series.

TL793.C649 2012
500.5—dc22
                                                    2011005134

Editorial Credits
Gillia Olson, editor; Lori Bye, designer; Wanda Winch, media researcher; Laura Manthe, production specialist

Photo Credits
Capstone Studio: Karon Dubke, 20, 21 (all); Constellation image from Firmamentum Sobiescianum sive Uranographia
by Johannes Hevelius, courtesy of the United State Naval Observatory and the Space Telescope Science Institute's
Office of Public Outreach, 5 (illustration); Dreamstime: Igor Sokalski, 5 (star field); Getty Images Inc: Hulton Archive,
7; NASA, 10, 11, 19, Johnson Space Center, 13, JPL, 14, 15, JPL/Cornell University, 17; Newscom: akg-images/RIA
Nowosti, 9; Shutterstock: Carsten Reisinger, cover, Giovanni Benintende, 1

Note to Parents and Teachers

The Earth and Space Science series supports national science standards related to earth and
space science. This book describes and illustrates space exploration. The images support early
readers in understanding the text. The repetition of words and phrases helps early readers learn
new words. This book also introduces early readers to subject-specific vocabulary words, which
are defined in the Glossary section. Early readers may need assistance to read some words and to
use the Table of Contents, Glossary, Read More, Internet Sites, and Index sections of the book.

Printed in the United States of America in North Mankato, Minnesota.
032011   006110CGF11

Table of Contents

Looking Up 4

Telescopes 6

Satellites 8

People in Space 10

Moon Landing 12

Probes 14

Robots 16

The Future 18

Make a Balloon Rocket 20

Glossary 22

Read More 23

Internet Sites 23

Index 24

Looking Up

Since time began, people

have watched the skies.

Thousands of years ago,

people named groups of stars,

called constellations.

Telescopes

In 1609 Galileo became the first person to look at space with a telescope. He discovered that the moon wasn't smooth. It is bumpy and uneven.

Satellites

In the 1900s people built
rockets to send into space.
In 1957 Russia launched
the first satellite into space.
It was called *Sputnik*.

Sputnik

9

People in Space

Before people went into space,
scientists sent a dog and
a chimpanzee. Finally, in 1961,
Yuri Gagarin became the first
person in space.

Yuri Gagarin

Ham, the
first chimpanzee
in space

11

Moon Landing

The next stop was the moon.

In 1969 Neil Armstrong took

the first steps on the moon.

Buzz Aldrin followed.

They placed an American flag.

Probes

People soon sent probes to learn about the planets. In 1977 the *Voyager* probes launched. They took pictures of Jupiter, Saturn, Neptune, and Uranus.

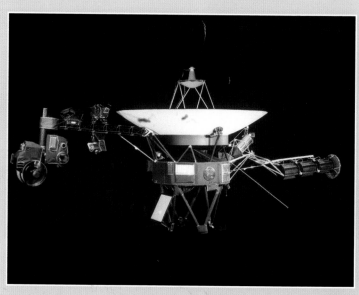

Voyager I

Jupiter

Saturn

Uranus Neptune

Earth

Robots

Robots also help explore space. Two rovers landed on Mars in 2004. People controlled them from Earth. The rovers found that Mars likely once had water.

The Future

In the future, astronauts want

to go beyond the moon. Mars

may be the next stop in space.

Where would you explore,

if you could travel in space?

Make a Balloon Rocket

Make a balloon rocket at home! Instead of rocket fuel, air will send your rocket into the sky!

You will need:
- long, thin balloon
- drinking straw
- rubber band

1. Blow up the balloon and let the air out of it several times to stretch it out. Have an adult help, if needed.

2. With no air in the balloon, insert the straw halfway into the balloon.

3. Loop the rubber band around the straw and balloon to hold the straw in place. Do it as tightly as you can.

4. Blow up the balloon by blowing into the straw.

5. When you're done, hold your finger over the end of the straw to trap the air.

6. Hold the balloon away from you and lightly push the balloon up as you let go. Watch your rocket go!

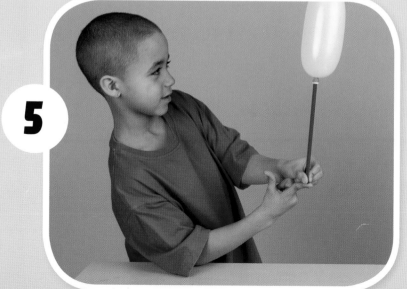

Glossary

constellation—a group of stars; constellations are often thought to look like animals, people, or objects

launch—to send a rocket or spacecraft into space

probe—a tool or device used to study or explore something

rocket—a vehicle usually shaped like a tube with a pointed end; rockets move by pushing fuel from one end

rover—a small vehicle often moved by remote control

satellite—a spacecraft that circles Earth; satellites gather and send information

telescope—a tool that makes objects look closer than they really are

Read More

Bowman, Donna H. *What Is the Moon Made Of? And Other Questions Kids Have about Space.* Kids' Questions. Minneapolis: Picture Window Books, 2010.

Braun, Eric. *If I Were an Astronaut.* Dream Big! Minneapolis: Picture Window Books, 2010.

Zappa, Marcia. *Constellations.* The Universe. Edina, Minn.: ABDO Pub., 2011.

Internet Sites

FactHound offers a safe, fun way to find Internet sites related to this book. All of the sites on FactHound have been researched by our staff.

Here's all you do:

Visit *www.facthound.com*

Type in this code: 9781429668101

Check out projects, games and lots more at
www.capstonekids.com

Index

Aldrin, Buzz, 12

Armstrong, Neil, 12

chimpanzees, 10

constellations, 4

dogs, 10

first person in space, 10

future space travel, 18

Galileo, 6

Gagarin, Yuri, 10

Mars, 16, 18

moon, 6, 18

    landing on, 12

planets, 14, 16, 18

probes, 14

robots, 16

rockets, 8

Russia, 8

satellites, 8

Sputnik, 8

stars, 4

telescopes, 6

Voyager, 14

Word Count: 194

Grade: 1

Early-Intervention Level: 22